W9-CIL-550

CHRISTMAS
Cookies for Kids

Publications International, Ltd.
Favorite Brand Name Recipes at www.fbnr.com

Copyright © 2001 Publications International, Ltd.
All rights reserved. This publication may not be reproduced or quoted in whole or in part by any means whatsoever without written permission from:

Louis Weber, CEO
Publications International, Ltd.
7373 North Cicero Avenue
Lincolnwood, IL 60712

Permission is never granted for commercial purposes.

All recipes and photographs that contain specific brand names are copyrighted by those companies and/or associations, unless otherwise specified. All photographs *except* those on pages 11, 33, 39, 47 and 59 copyright © Publications International, Ltd.

DOLE® is a registered trademark of Dole Food Company, Inc.

™/© M&M's, M and the M&M's Characters are trademarks of Mars, Incorporated.
© Mars, Inc. 2001.

Albers, Libby's, Nestlé and Toll House are registered trademarks of Nestlé.

Some of the products listed in this publication may be in limited distribution.

Pictured on the front cover: Decadent Brownies *(page 29)*, Jolly Peanut Butter Gingerbread Cookies *(page 35)*, Almond Milk Chocolate Chippers *(page 51)*, Yuletide Linzer Bars *(page 28)*, Mocha Crinkles *(page 29)*, Peanut Butter Chocolate Chippers *(page 55)* and Candy Cane Cookies *(page 50)*.

Pictured on the back cover *(clockwise from top):* Chocolate Mint Ravioli Cookies *(page 36)*, White Chocolate Squares *(page 26)* and Ice Skates *(page 56)*.

ISBN: 0-7853-5582-0

Manufactured in China.

8 7 6 5 4 3 2 1

Microwave Cooking: Microwave ovens vary in wattage. Use the cooking times as guidelines and check for doneness before adding more time.

Preparation/Cooking Times: Preparation times are based on the approximate amount of time required to assemble the recipe before cooking, baking, chilling or serving. These times include preparation steps such as measuring, chopping and mixing. The fact that some preparations and cooking can be done simultaneously is taken into account. Preparation of optional ingredients and serving suggestions is not included.

CHRISTMAS
Cookies for Kids

Christmas Cookies 101

No other treat captures the spirit of the holidays like Christmas cookies. The stir of a wooden spoon, the shaping of each delicious tidbit, the carefully timed precision of baking sheets in and out of the oven—they all culminate in the creation of the perfect mouthful of Christmas cheer. Fill your home with the joyful, sweet aroma of baking cookies this holiday season.

BAKING BASICS

Take the guesswork out of cookie baking by practicing the following techniques:

◆ Read the entire recipe before you begin to make sure you have all the necessary ingredients and baking utensils.

◆ Remove butter, margarine and cream cheese from the refrigerator to soften, if necessary.

◆ Toast and chop nuts, pare and slice fruit, and melt chocolate before preparing the cookie dough.

◆ Measure all the ingredients accurately and assemble them in the order they are called for in the recipe.

◆ When making bar cookies or brownies, use the pan size specified in the recipe.

◆ Prepare the pans according to the recipe directions. Adjust oven racks and preheat the oven.

SMART COOKIE TIPS

◆ The best cookie sheets to use are those with little or no sides. They allow the heat to circulate easily during baking and promote even browning.

◆ Use shiny cookie sheets for the best baking results. Dark cookie sheets will cause the bottoms of the cookies to be dark.

◆ If a recipe calls for greasing cookie sheets, use shortening or vegetable cooking spray for best results. Line cookie sheets with parchment paper as an alternative to greasing. This cuts cleanup, bakes cookies more evenly and allows them to cool right on the paper instead of on wire racks.

◆ For more consistent baking and browning, place only one cookie sheet at a time in the center of the oven. If the heat distribution in your oven is uneven, rotate the cookie sheet halfway through the baking time. Also, if you do use more than one sheet at a time, move the cookie sheets from top to bottom oven racks halfway through the baking time.

◆ Most cookies bake quickly and should be watched carefully to avoid overbaking. Check them at the minimum baking time, then watch carefully to make sure they don't burn. It is generally better to slightly underbake rather than to overbake cookies.

◆ Allow cookie sheets to cool between batches; the dough will spread if placed on a hot cookie sheet.

S P R E A D   O U T

Using the appropriate type of fat in a cookie recipe will ensure the best results. When a recipe calls for butter or margarine, avoid using margarine-type products marked as "spreads" or those that come in tubs; their higher water content can create undesirable results. If you use margarine, use only stick products labeled as margarine.

Holiday Cookie Exchange

Give your Christmas a new twist by hosting an old-fashioned cookie exchange. It's a delicious way to share the holiday spirit. Ask guests to bring a batch or two of their favorite cookies. You might also ask them to bring copies of their recipe to share. That way, if other guests like what they've tasted, they can bake the cookies too. As the host, you simply provide bags, baskets or plates for collecting and carrying all the cookies, and a few beverages to accompany the cookie feast. Place all the cookies on a table and have everybody take some of each kind home for holiday guests.

The Name Game

The word cookie comes from the Dutch word *koekje* meaning "little cake." The Dutch brought these little cakes to their first settlements in America, and they have been popular ever since. With so many flavors, shapes and sizes to choose from, cookies have definitely earned their place as America's favorite snack food.

SPECIAL DELIVERY

When those you love can't join you for the holidays, send some Christmas their way by mailing cookies. Prepare soft, moist cookies that can handle jostling rather than fragile, brittle cookies that might crumble. Brownies and bar cookies are generally sturdy, but avoid shipping those with moist fillings and frostings, since they become sticky at room temperature. For the same reason, shipping anything with chocolate during the summer or to warm climates is also risky. Wrap each type of cookie separately to retain flavors and textures. Cookies can also be wrapped back-to-back in pairs with either plastic wrap or foil. Bar cookies should be packed in layers the size of the container. Place wrapped cookies as tightly as possible in snug rows inside a sturdy shipping box or container. Fill the bottom of the shipping container with an even layer of packing material. Do not use popped popcorn or puffed cereal as it may attract insects. Place crumpled waxed paper, newspaper or paper toweling in between layers of wrapped cookies. Fill any crevices with packing material, and add a final layer at the top of the box. Ship the container to arrive as soon as possible.

COOKIE LINGO

The seemingly endless variety of cookies can actually be divided into five basic types: bar, drop, refrigerator (slice and bake), rolled and shaped. These types are determined by the consistency of the dough and how it is formed into cookies.

Cookie Exchange

Chocolate Mint Sugar Cookie Drops

- 2½ **cups all-purpose flour**
- 1½ **teaspoons baking powder**
- ¾ **teaspoon salt**
- 1 **cup granulated sugar**
- ¾ **cup vegetable oil**
- 1 **teaspoon vanilla extract**
- 2 **eggs**
- 1½ **cups (10-ounce package) NESTLÉ® TOLL HOUSE® Mint Chocolate Morsels**
- **Red and green coarse sugar or additional granulated sugar (optional)**

Combine flour, baking powder and salt in small bowl; set aside.

Combine 1 cup granulated sugar, oil and vanilla in large bowl. Add eggs, 1 at a time, beating well after each addition. Gradually beat in flour mixture. Stir in morsels. Shape rounded teaspoonfuls of dough into 1-inch balls. Roll in coarse sugar or additional granulated sugar. Place on ungreased baking sheets.

Bake in preheated 350°F. oven for 7 to 9 minutes or until centers are just set. Let stand 2 minutes; remove to wire racks to cool completely.

Makes about 5½ dozen cookies

Top to bottom: Fudgy Cheesecake Swirl Brownies (page 15) and Chocolate Mint Sugar Cookie Drops

Magic Make It Your Way Drop Cookies

3 cups sifted all-purpose
flour
3 teaspoons baking powder
¾ teaspoon salt
¾ cup (1½ sticks) butter or
margarine, softened
2 eggs
1 teaspoon vanilla extract
1 (14-ounce) can EAGLE®
BRAND Sweetened
Condensed Milk (NOT
evaporated milk)
One "favorite" ingredient
(see below)

1. Preheat oven to 350°F.
Grease baking sheets; set aside.
In large bowl, sift together dry
ingredients. Stir in butter, eggs,
vanilla and **Eagle Brand.** Fold
in one of your "favorite"
ingredients.

2. Drop by level teaspoonfuls,
about 2 inches apart, onto
prepared baking sheets. Bake
8 to 10 minutes or until edges
are slightly browned. Remove
at once from baking sheet.
Cool. Store covered at room
temperature.

Makes about 4 dozen cookies

*"Make it your way" with your
favorite ingredient (pick one):*

- 1 (6-ounce) package semi-sweet chocolate chips

- 1½ cups raisins

- 1½ cups cornflakes

- 1½ cups toasted shredded coconut

Helpful Hint

*To easily shape drop
cookies into a uniform size,
use an ice cream scoop
with a release bar. The
bar usually has a number
on it indicating the
number of scoops that can
be made from one quart
of ice cream. The handiest
scoop sizes for cookies
are #40, #50
and #80.*

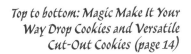

*Top to bottom: Magic Make It Your
Way Drop Cookies and Versatile
Cut-Out Cookies (page 14)*

Versatile Cut-Out Cookies

3⅓ cups all-purpose flour
1 tablespoon baking powder
½ teaspoon salt
1 (14-ounce) can EAGLE® BRAND Sweetened Condensed Milk (NOT evaporated milk)
¾ cup (1½ sticks) butter or margarine, softened
2 eggs
2 teaspoons vanilla or 1½ teaspoons almond or lemon extract
Ready-to-spread frosting

1. Preheat oven to 350°F. Grease baking sheets; set aside. In medium bowl, combine flour, baking powder and salt; set aside. In large bowl, beat **Eagle Brand,** butter, eggs and vanilla until well blended. Add dry ingredients; mix well.

2. On floured surface, lightly knead dough to form smooth ball. Divide into thirds. On well-floured surface, roll out each portion to ⅛-inch thickness. Cut with floured cookie cutter. Place 1 inch apart on prepared sheets.

3. Bake 7 to 9 minutes or until lightly browned around edges. Cool completely. Frost and decorate as desired. Store loosely covered at room temperature.
Makes about 6½ dozen cookies

Prep Time: 15 minutes
Bake Time: 7 to 9 minutes

Sandwich Cookies: Use 2½-inch cookie cutter. Bake as directed above. Sandwich two cookies together with ready-to-spread frosting. Sprinkle with powdered sugar or colored sugar if desired.

Helpful Hint

Store soft and crisp cookies separately at room temperature to prevent changes in texture and flavor. Keep soft cookies in airtight containers. Store crisp cookies in containers with loose-fitting lids to prevent moisture buildup.

Fudgy Cheesecake Swirl Brownies

¾ **cup (1½ sticks) butter or margarine**
2 **bars (2 ounces *each*) NESTLÉ® TOLL HOUSE® Unsweetened Chocolate Baking Bars**
2¼ **cups granulated sugar, divided**
4 **eggs**
1¾ **cups all-purpose flour**
1 **package (8 ounces) cream cheese, softened**
1 **teaspoon vanilla extract**

MELT butter and baking bars in medium, heavy-duty saucepan over low heat, stirring until smooth. Cool to room temperature. Stir in 1¾ cups sugar. Beat in 3 eggs; stir in flour. Spread into greased 13×9-inch baking pan.

BEAT cream cheese and remaining ½ cup sugar. Beat in remaining egg and vanilla. Pour over chocolate mixture; deeply swirl batters with knife.

BAKE in preheated 350°F. oven for 30 to 35 minutes or until wooden pick inserted near center comes out slightly sticky. Cool completely in pan on wire rack.   *Makes 2 dozen brownies*

Helpful Hint

When making brownies or bar cookies, line the pan with foil and leave a 2-inch overhang on the sides. Grease the foil if the recipe directs. After the brownies cool, just lift them out of the pan using the foil handles. Not only will this save on cleanup time, but you'll avoid marking up your pan when cutting the brownies.

Peanut Butter Spritz Sandwiches

1 package DUNCAN HINES® Peanut Butter Cookie Mix
¼ cup vegetable oil
1 egg
4 bars (1.55 ounces each) milk chocolate

1. Preheat oven to 375°F.

2. Combine cookie mix, peanut butter packet from mix, oil and egg in large bowl. Stir until thoroughly blended. Fill cookie press with dough. Press desired shapes 2 inches apart onto ungreased baking sheet. Bake at 375°F for 7 to 9 minutes or until set but not browned. Cool 1 minute on baking sheet.

3. Cut each chocolate bar into 12 sections. To assemble, gently remove one cookie from baking sheet. Place one milk chocolate bar section on bottom of warm cookie; top with second cookie. Press together. Repeat with remaining cookies. Place cookies on wire rack until chocolate is set.

Makes 3½ to 4 dozen sandwich cookies

Holiday Almond Wreaths

¾ cup FLEISCHMANN'S® Margarine, softened
½ cup sugar
¼ cup EGG BEATERS® Healthy Real Egg Product
1 teaspoon almond extract
2 cups all-purpose flour
½ cup ground almonds
Green and red glacé cherries, optional

Preheat oven to 400°F. In medium bowl, using electric mixer at medium speed, cream margarine and sugar. Add Egg Beaters® and almond extract. Stir in flour and ground almonds. Using pastry bag with ½-inch star tip, pipe dough into 1-inch wreaths 2 inches apart on ungreased cookie sheets. Decorate wreaths with green and red glacé cherries, if desired. Bake for 10 to 12 minutes or until golden brown. Cool on wire racks.

Makes about 3 dozen cookies

Cocoa-Walnut Crescents

1 cup (2 sticks) butter or margarine, softened
⅔ cup powdered sugar
⅓ cup HERSHEY'S Cocoa
1 teaspoon vanilla extract
⅛ teaspoon salt
1⅔ cups all-purpose flour
1 cup walnuts, finely chopped
1⅔ cups (10-ounce package) HERSHEY'S Premier White Chips
1 tablespoon shortening (do *not* use butter, margarine, spread or oil)
1 cup HERSHEY'S Semi-Sweet Chocolate Chips, melted

1. Beat butter and sugar in large bowl until fluffy. Add cocoa, vanilla and salt; mix on low speed until blended. Mix in flour and walnuts. Cover; refrigerate dough 1 hour.

2. Heat oven to 325°F. Grease cookie sheet. Divide dough into 6 portions. Working with one portion at a time, shape into 18-inch long rope; cut into 12 (1½-inch) pieces. Form into crescent shapes, tapering ends. Place on cookie sheet. Repeat with remaining dough.

3. Bake 15 to 18 minutes. Remove from cookie sheet to wire rack; cool completely.

4. Place white chips and shortening in microwave-safe bowl. Microwave at HIGH (100%) 1 minute or until chips are softened; stir. Microwave at HIGH an additional 15 seconds at a time, stirring after each heating, just until chips are melted when stirred.

5. Dip crescents halfway into melted white chips; place on wax paper until set. Drizzle coated ends of crescents with melted semi-sweet chips. Allow to stand until set.
Makes about 6 dozen cookies

Candy Bar Bars

¾ cup (1½ sticks) butter or
    margarine, softened
¼ cup peanut butter
1 cup packed brown sugar
1 teaspoon baking soda
2 cups quick-cooking oats
1½ cups all-purpose flour
1 egg
1 (14-ounce) can EAGLE®
    BRAND Sweetened
    Condensed Milk (NOT
    evaporated milk)
4 cups chopped candy bars
    (such as chocolate-
    coated caramel-topped
    nougat bars with
    peanuts, chocolate-
    covered crisp wafers,
    chocolate-covered
    caramel-topped cookie
    bars, or chocolate-
    covered peanut butter
    cups)

1. Preheat oven to 350°F. In large bowl, combine butter and peanut butter. Add sugar and baking soda; beat well. Stir in oats and flour. Reserve 1¾ cups crumb mixture.

2. Stir egg into remaining crumb mixture; press firmly on bottom of ungreased 15×10×1-inch baking pan. Bake 15 minutes.

3. Spread **Eagle Brand** over baked crust. Stir together reserved crumb mixture and candy bar pieces; sprinkle evenly over top. Bake 25 minutes or until golden. Cool. Cut into bars. Store covered at room temperature. *Makes 48 bars*

Prep Time: 20 minutes
Bake Time: 40 minutes

Helpful Hint

Try cutting bar cookies into triangles or diamonds for a festive new shape. To make diamonds, cut straight lines 1 to 1½ inches apart down the length of the bars. Then, diagonally cut straight lines 1 to 1½ inches apart across the bars.

Mint Chocolate Pinwheels

1¼ cups all-purpose flour
1 teaspoon baking powder
½ teaspoon salt
⅔ cup butter, softened
1 cup sugar
1 large egg
1 teaspoon vanilla
1 cup uncooked quick-
   cooking oats
1 cup mint chocolate chips

1. Stir together flour, baking powder and salt in small bowl. Beat butter and sugar in large bowl until light and fluffy. Add egg and vanilla; beat well. Gradually add flour mixture. Beat at low speed. Stir in oats.

2. Place chocolate chips in 1-cup glass measure. Microwave at HIGH about 2 minutes or until melted, stirring after 1½ minutes. Divide cookie dough in half. Add melted chocolate to one half; mix well.

3. Roll out each half of dough between 2 sheets of waxed paper into 15×10-inch rectangles. Remove waxed paper from top of each rectangle.

4. Place chocolate dough over plain dough; remove bottom sheet of waxed paper from bottom of chocolate dough. Starting at long side, tightly roll up dough jelly-roll fashion, removing waxed paper as you roll. Wrap dough in plastic wrap; refrigerate at least 2 hours or up to 24 hours.

5. Preheat oven to 350°F. Lightly grease cookie sheet; set aside.

6. Unwrap log. Cut dough into ¼-inch slices. Place 3 inches apart on prepared cookie sheets.

7. Bake 10 to 12 minutes or until set. Remove cookies with spatula to wire racks; cool completely. Store tightly covered at room temperature or freeze up to 3 months.
   Makes about 3 dozen cookies

Holiday Pineapple Cheese Bars

¼ cup butter or margarine
¼ cup packed brown sugar
¾ cup flour
¾ cup finely chopped
     macadamia nuts
1 can (8 ounces) crushed
     pineapple, undrained
1 package (8 ounces)
     PHILADELPHIA®
     Cream Cheese,
     softened
¼ cup granulated sugar
1 egg
1 cup BAKER'S® ANGEL
     FLAKE® Coconut
½ cup coarsely chopped
     macadamia nuts
1 tablespoon butter or
     margarine, melted

PREHEAT oven to 350°F.

BEAT ¼ cup butter and brown sugar in small mixing bowl at medium speed with electric mixer until well blended. Add flour and ¾ cup finely chopped nuts; mix well. Press onto bottom of 9-inch square baking pan. Bake 10 minutes. Cool.

DRAIN pineapple, reserving 2 tablespoons liquid.

BEAT cream cheese, reserved liquid, granulated sugar and egg in small mixing bowl at medium speed with electric mixer until well blended. Stir in pineapple. Pour over crust.

SPRINKLE with combined coconut, coarsely chopped nuts and 1 tablespoon butter.

BAKE 18 minutes. Cool completely. Cut into bars.
Makes about 1½ dozen bars

Prep Time: 20 minutes
Bake Time: 18 minutes

Helpful Hint

Cool most bar cookies in the pan on a wire rack until barely warm, then cut into bars or squares. For easy serving, remove a corner piece first; then remove the rest.

Basic Banana Holiday Cookies

2¾ cups all-purpose flour
1 teaspoon baking soda
¼ teaspoon salt
1 cup margarine, softened
1¼ cups granulated sugar, divided
¼ cup packed brown sugar
1 large, ripe DOLE® Banana, mashed (about ½ cup)
1 egg
½ teaspoon ground cinnamon

- **Combine** flour, baking soda and salt in medium bowl; set aside.

- **Beat** together margarine, 1 cup granulated sugar and brown sugar in large bowl until creamy. Beat in banana and egg until blended. Stir in flour mixture until combined. Cover; chill 2 hours or until dough is firm enough to handle.

- **Combine** remaining ¼ cup granulated sugar and cinnamon in small bowl.

- **Shape** dough into 1-inch balls. Roll in cinnamon mixture; place two inches apart on ungreased baking sheets.

- **Bake** at 350°F 10 to 12 minutes or until lightly browned. Carefully remove cookies to wire rack to cool completely.

Makes 4½ dozen cookies

Prep Time: 15 minutes
Bake Time: 12 minutes

Chocolate Banana Stars: Prepare, shape and bake dough as directed except roll dough in 1 cup finely chopped DOLE® Almonds instead of cinnamon mixture. Immediately after baking, press unwrapped individual milk chocolate star candies into center of each cookie. Cool as directed.

Banana Chippers: Prepare and shape dough as directed except stir in 1 package (10 ounces) peanut butter chips and 1 cup chopped pecans or walnuts into dough and omit cinnamon mixture. Bake and cool as directed.

Simple & Sweet

Choco-Scutterbotch

⅔ **Butter Flavor CRISCO®**
    Stick or ⅔ cup Butter
    Flavor CRISCO® all-
    vegetable shortening
½ **cup packed brown sugar**
 2 **eggs**
 1 **package (18¼ ounces)**
    deluxe yellow cake mix
 1 **cup toasted rice cereal**
½ **cup butterscotch chips**
½ **cup milk chocolate**
    chunks
½ **cup semisweet chocolate**
    chips
½ **cup coarsely chopped**
    walnuts or pecans

1. Heat oven to 375°F. Place sheets of foil on countertop.

2. Combine shortening and brown sugar. Beat at medium speed with electric mixer until well blended. Beat in eggs.

3. Add cake mix slowly at low speed until well blended. Stir in cereal, butterscotch chips, chocolate chunks and chips, and nuts until blended.

4. Roll into 1¼-inch balls. Put 2 inches apart on *ungreased* baking sheet. Flatten slightly.

5. Bake 7 to 9 minutes or until just brown around edges. *Do not overbake.* Cool 2 minutes on baking sheet. Remove cookies to foil to cool completely.
Makes 3 dozen cookies

Coconut Macaroons

1 (14-ounce) can EAGLE®
    BRAND Sweetened
    Condensed Milk (NOT
    evaporated milk)
2 teaspoons vanilla extract
1 to 1½ teaspoons almond
    extract
2 (7-ounce) packages
    flaked coconut
    (5⅓ cups)

1. Preheat oven to 325°F. Line baking sheets with foil; grease and flour foil. Set aside.

2. In large bowl, combine **Eagle Brand,** vanilla and almond extract. Stir in coconut. Drop by rounded teaspoons onto prepared sheets; with spoon, slightly flatten each mound.

3. Bake 15 to 17 minutes or until golden. Remove from baking sheets; cool on wire rack. Store loosely covered at room temperature.
    Makes about 4 dozen cookies

Prep Time: 10 minutes
Bake Time: 15 to 17 minutes

White Chocolate Squares

1 (12-ounce) package
    white chocolate chips,
    divided
¼ cup (½ stick) butter or
    margarine
2 cups all-purpose flour
½ teaspoon baking powder
1 (14-ounce) can EAGLE®
    BRAND Sweetened
    Condensed Milk (NOT
    evaporated milk)
1 cup chopped pecans,
    toasted
1 large egg
1 teaspoon vanilla extract
    Powdered sugar

1. Preheat oven to 350°F. Grease 13×9-inch baking pan. In large saucepan over low heat, melt 1 cup chips and butter. Stir in flour and baking powder until blended. Stir in **Eagle Brand,** pecans, egg, vanilla and remaining chips. Spoon mixture into prepared pan.

2. Bake 20 to 25 minutes. Cool. Sprinkle with powdered sugar; cut into squares. Store covered at room temperature.
    Makes 24 bars

Yuletide Linzer Bars

1⅓ cups butter, softened
¾ cup sugar
1 egg
1 teaspoon grated lemon
   peel
2½ cups all-purpose flour
1½ cups whole almonds,
   ground
1 teaspoon ground
   cinnamon
¾ cup raspberry preserves
   Powdered sugar

Preheat oven to 350°F. Grease
13×9-inch baking pan.

Beat butter and sugar in large
bowl with electric mixer until
creamy. Beat in egg and lemon
peel until blended. Mix in flour,
almonds and cinnamon until
well blended.

Press 2 cups dough into
bottom of prepared pan.
Spread preserves over crust.
Press remaining dough, a bit at
a time, evenly over preserves.

Bake 35 to 40 minutes until
golden brown. Cool in pan on
wire rack. Sprinkle with
powdered sugar; cut into bars.
Makes 36 bars

No-Bake Peanutty Cookies

2 cups Roasted Honey Nut
   SKIPPY® Creamy or
   SUPER CHUNK®
   Peanut Butter
2 cups graham cracker
   crumbs
1 cup confectioners' sugar
½ cup KARO® Light or
   Dark Corn Syrup
¼ cup semisweet chocolate
   chips, melted
   Colored sprinkles
   (optional)

1. In large bowl, combine
peanut butter, graham cracker
crumbs, confectioners' sugar
and corn syrup. Mix until
smooth.

2. Shape into 1-inch balls.
Place on waxed paper-lined
cookie sheets.

3. Drizzle melted chocolate
over balls; roll in colored
sprinkles if desired. Store
covered in refrigerator.
Makes about 5 dozen cookies

Decadent Brownies

½ cup dark corn syrup
½ cup butter
6 squares (1 ounce each) semisweet chocolate
¾ cup sugar
3 eggs
1 cup all-purpose flour
1 cup chopped walnuts
1 teaspoon vanilla
   Fudge Glaze (recipe follows)

Preheat oven to 350°F. Grease 8-inch square pan. Combine corn syrup, butter and chocolate in large heavy saucepan. Place over low heat; stir until chocolate is melted and ingredients are blended. Remove from heat; blend in sugar. Stir in eggs, flour, walnuts and vanilla. Spread batter evenly in prepared pan. Bake 20 to 25 minutes or just until center is set. *Do not overbake.* Meanwhile, prepare Fudge Glaze. Remove brownies from oven. Immediately spread glaze evenly over hot brownies. Cool in pan on wire rack. Cut into 2-inch squares.

Makes 16 brownies

Fudge Glaze

3 squares (1 ounce each) semisweet chocolate
2 tablespoons dark corn syrup
1 tablespoon butter or margarine
1 teaspoon light cream or milk

Combine chocolate, corn syrup and butter in small heavy saucepan. Stir over low heat until chocolate is melted; mix in cream.

Helpful Hint

Bar cookies and brownies are some of the easiest cookies to make—simply mix the batter, spread in the pan and bake. These cookies are also quick to prepare since they bake all at once rather than in batches on a cookie sheet.

Mocha Crinkles

1⅓ cups firmly packed light
    brown sugar
½ cup vegetable oil
¼ cup low-fat sour cream
1 egg
1 teaspoon vanilla
1¾ cups all-purpose flour
¾ cup unsweetened cocoa
    powder
2 teaspoons instant
    espresso or coffee
    granules
1 teaspoon baking soda
¼ teaspoon salt
⅛ teaspoon black pepper
½ cup powdered sugar

1. Beat brown sugar and oil in medium bowl with electric mixer. Mix in sour cream, egg and vanilla. Set aside.

2. Mix flour, cocoa, espresso, baking soda, salt and pepper in another medium bowl.

3. Add flour mixture to brown sugar mixture; mix well. Refrigerate dough until firm, 3 to 4 hours.

4. Preheat oven to 350°F. Pour powdered sugar into shallow bowl. Set aside. Cut dough into 1-inch pieces; roll into balls. Roll balls in powdered sugar.

5. Bake on ungreased cookie sheets 10 to 12 minutes or until tops of cookies are firm to touch. (Do not overbake.) Cool on wire racks.

Makes 72 cookies

No-Bake Cherry Crisps

¼ cup butter, softened
1 cup powdered sugar
1 cup peanut butter
1⅓ cups crisp rice cereal
½ cup maraschino cherries,
    drained, dried and
    chopped
¼ cup plus 2 tablespoons
    mini semisweet
    chocolate chips
¼ cup chopped pecans
1 to 2 cups flaked coconut
    (for rolling)

In large bowl, beat butter, sugar and peanut butter. Stir in cereal, cherries, chips and pecans. Mix well. Shape teaspoonfuls of dough into 1-inch balls. Roll in coconut. Place on cookie sheets and chill in refrigerator 1 hour.

Makes about 3 dozen cookies

Pinwheel Cookies

½ **cup shortening plus additional for greasing**
⅓ **cup plus 1 tablespoon butter, softened and divided**
2 **egg yolks**
½ **teaspoon vanilla**
1 **package DUNCAN HINES® Moist Deluxe Fudge Marble Cake Mix**

1. Combine ½ cup shortening, ⅓ cup butter, egg yolks and vanilla in large bowl. Mix at low speed of electric mixer until blended. Set aside cocoa packet from cake mix. Gradually add cake mix. Blend well.

2. Divide dough in half. Add cocoa packet and remaining 1 tablespoon butter to one half of dough. Knead until well blended and chocolate colored.

3. Roll out yellow dough between two pieces of waxed paper into 18×12×⅛-inch rectangle. Repeat for chocolate dough. Remove top pieces of waxed paper from chocolate and yellow dough. Lay yellow dough directly on top of chocolate. Remove remaining layers of waxed paper. Roll up jelly roll fashion, beginning at wide side. Refrigerate 2 hours.

4. Preheat oven to 350°F. Grease cookie sheets.

5. Cut dough into ⅛-inch slices. Place sliced dough 1 inch apart on prepared cookie sheets. Bake 9 to 11 minutes or until lightly browned. Cool 5 minutes on cookie sheets. Remove to cooling racks.

Makes about 3½ dozen cookies

Helpful Hint

Always cool cookies completely before stacking and storing.

Chocolate Bursts

**6 squares (1 ounce each)
  semisweet chocolate**
**½ cup (1 stick) I CAN'T
  BELIEVE IT'S NOT
  BUTTER!® Spread**
¾ cup sugar
2 eggs
⅓ cup all-purpose flour
**¼ cup unsweetened cocoa
  powder**
1½ teaspoons vanilla extract
1 teaspoon baking powder
¼ teaspoon salt
**2 cups coarsely chopped
  pecans or walnuts**
**1 cup semisweet chocolate
  chips**

Preheat oven to 325°F. Grease baking sheets; set aside.

In medium microwave-safe bowl, heat chocolate squares and I Can't Believe It's Not Butter! Spread on HIGH (Full Power) 1 to 2 minutes or until chocolate is almost melted. Stir until completely melted.

In large bowl, with electric mixer, beat sugar and eggs until light and ribbony, about 2 minutes. Beat in chocolate mixture, flour, cocoa, vanilla, baking powder and salt, scraping side occasionally, until well blended. Stir in nuts and chocolate chips. Drop dough by rounded tablespoonfuls onto prepared sheets, about 2 inches apart.

Bake 15 minutes or until cookies are just set. On wire rack, let stand 2 minutes; remove from sheets and cool completely.

Makes about 3 dozen cookies

Helpful Hint

An easy way to dress up simple drop cookies is to drizzle them with melted chocolate or sprinkle them with powdered sugar after they are completely cooled. Before decorating, place waxed paper under the wire rack to make cleanup easier.

Jolly Peanut Butter Gingerbread Cookies

1⅔ cups (10-ounce package) REESE'S® Peanut Butter Chips
¾ cup (1½ sticks) butter or margarine, softened
1 cup packed light brown sugar
1 cup dark corn syrup
2 eggs
5 cups all-purpose flour
1 teaspoon baking soda
½ teaspoon ground cinnamon
¼ teaspoon ground ginger
¼ teaspoon salt

1. Place peanut butter chips in small microwave-safe bowl. Microwave at HIGH (100%) 1 to 2 minutes or until chips are melted when stirred. Beat melted peanut butter chips and butter in large bowl until well blended. Add brown sugar, corn syrup and eggs; beat until fluffy. Stir together flour, baking soda, cinnamon, ginger and salt. Add half of flour mixture to butter mixture; beat on low speed of mixer until smooth. With wooden spoon, stir in remaining flour mixture until well blended. Divide into thirds; wrap each in plastic wrap. Refrigerate at least 1 hour or until dough is firm enough to roll.

2. Heat oven to 325°F.

3. Roll 1 dough portion at a time to ⅛-inch thickness on lightly floured surface; with floured cookie cutters, cut into holiday shapes. Place on ungreased cookie sheet.

4. Bake 10 to 12 minutes or until set and lightly browned. Cool slightly; remove from cookie sheet to wire rack. Cool completely. Frost and decorate as desired.

Makes about 6 dozen cookies

Chocolate Mint Ravioli Cookies

1 package (15 ounces)
    refrigerated pie crusts
1 bar (7 ounces) cookies
    'n' mint chocolate
    candy
1 egg
    Powdered sugar

1. Preheat oven to 400°F. Unfold 1 pie crust on lightly floured surface. Roll into 13-inch circle. Using 2½-inch cutters, cut pastry into 24 circles, rerolling scraps if necessary. Repeat with remaining pie crust.

2. Separate candy bar into pieces marked on bar. Cut each chocolate piece in half. Beat egg and 1 tablespoon water together in small bowl with fork. Brush half of pastry circles lightly with egg mixture. Place 1 piece of chocolate in center of circles (there will be some candy bar left over). Top with remaining pastry circles. Seal edges with tines of fork.

3. Place on ungreased baking sheets. Brush with egg mixture.

4. Bake 8 to 10 minutes or until golden brown. Remove from cookie sheets; cool completely on wire rack. Dust with powdered sugar.

Makes 2 dozen cookies

Prep & Cook Time: 30 minutes

Helpful Hint

To flour means to apply a light coating of flour to a food or piece of equipment. Rolling pins, biscuit cutters, cookie cutters and work surfaces are floured to prevent doughs from sticking to them.

Raspberry Almond Sandwich Cookies

1 package DUNCAN HINES® Golden Sugar Cookie Mix
1 egg
¼ cup vegetable oil
1 tablespoon water
¾ teaspoon almond extract
1⅓ cups sliced natural almonds, broken
Seedless red raspberry jam

Preheat oven to 375°F.

Combine cookie mix, egg, oil, water and almond extract in large bowl. Stir until thoroughly blended. Drop half of dough by level teaspoonfuls 2 inches apart onto *ungreased* cookie sheets. (Dough will spread during baking 1½ to 1¾ inches.)

Place almonds on waxed paper. Drop remaining half of dough by level teaspoonfuls onto nuts. Place almond side up 2 inches apart onto *ungreased* cookie sheets.

Bake both plain and almond cookies 6 minutes or until set but not browned. Cool 1 minute on cookie sheets. Remove to cooling racks. Cool completely.

Spread bottoms of plain cookies with jam; top with almond cookies. Press together to make sandwiches. Store in airtight container.

Makes 6 dozen sandwich cookies

Helpful Hint

When baking cookies, use the same amount of dough for each cookie. Cookies that are uniform in size and shape will finish baking at the same time.

Norwegian Wreaths

1 hard-cooked large egg
  yolk
1 large egg, separated
½ cup butter, softened
½ cup powdered sugar
½ teaspoon vanilla
1¼ cups all-purpose flour
  Coarse sugar crystals or
    crushed sugar cubes

1. Preheat oven to 350°F. Grease cookie sheets; set aside.

2. Beat cooked and raw egg yolks in medium bowl until smooth, reserving egg white. Beat in butter, powdered sugar and vanilla. Stir in 1 cup flour. Stir in additional flour until stiff dough forms.

3. Place dough on sheet of waxed paper. Using waxed paper to hold dough, roll it back and forth to form a log; cut into 18 equal pieces. Roll each piece of dough into an 8-inch rope, tapering ends.

4. Shape ropes into wreaths; overlap ends and let extend out from wreath. Place on prepared cookie sheets. Chill 15 minutes or until firm.

5. Beat reserved egg white with fork until foamy. Brush wreaths with egg white; sprinkle with sugar crystals. Bake 8 to 10 minutes or until light golden brown. Remove cookies to wire racks; cool completely.
Makes about 1½ dozen cookies

Kids' Favorites

Fireside Cookie

**1 package (18 ounces)
refrigerated cookie
dough, any flavor
All-purpose flour
(optional)
Icings, red licorice bites,
black string licorice,
gum drops and
assorted candies**

1. Preheat oven to 350°F.
Line large cookie sheet with
parchment paper.

2. Remove dough from wrapper
according to package directions.
Remove ¼ of dough. Roll into
strip about 12×3 inches. Trim
to 11×2¼ inches; set aside.

Roll remaining dough into
rectangle about 10×8 inches.
Trim to 9×7¾ inches; place on
prepared cookie sheet. Sprinkle
with flour to minimize sticking,
if necessary. Place reserved
strip of dough at top of
rectangle to make mantel. Roll
scraps and cut into stocking
shapes. Place on prepared
cookie sheet.

3. Bake 10 minutes or until
edges are lightly browned.
Cool on baking sheet 5 minutes.
Remove to wire rack; cool
completely.

4. Decorate with icings and
candies as shown, attaching
stockings to cookie with icing.
Makes 1 large cookie

Gingerbread People

2¼ cups all-purpose flour
2 teaspoons ground cinnamon
2 teaspoons ground ginger
1 teaspoon baking powder
½ teaspoon salt
¼ teaspoon ground cloves
¼ teaspoon ground nutmeg
¾ cup butter, softened
½ cup packed light brown sugar
½ cup dark molasses
1 egg
Icing (recipe follows)
Candies and other decorations (optional)

1. Combine flour, cinnamon, ginger, baking powder, salt, cloves and nutmeg in large bowl.

2. Beat butter and brown sugar in large bowl until light and fluffy. Beat in molasses and egg. Gradually add flour mixture; beat until well blended. Shape dough into 3 disks. Wrap well in plastic wrap; refrigerate 1 hour or until firm.

3. Preheat oven to 350°F. Working with 1 disk at a time, place on lightly floured surface.

Roll out dough with lightly floured rolling pin to ¼-inch thickness. Cut out gingerbread people with floured 5-inch cookie cutters; place on ungreased cookie sheets. Press dough trimmings together gently; reroll and cut out more cookies.

4. Bake about 12 minutes or until edges are golden brown. Let cookies stand on cookie sheets 1 minute; remove to wire racks to cool completely.

5. Prepare Icing and pipe onto cooled cookies. Decorate with candies, if desired. Let stand at room temperature 20 minutes or until set. Store tightly covered at room temperature.

Makes about 16 large cookies

Icing

2 cups powdered sugar
2 tablespoons milk
Food coloring (optional)

Place powdered sugar and milk in small bowl; stir with spoon until smooth. (Icing will be very thick. If it is too thick, stir in 1 teaspoon additional milk.) Divide into small bowls and tint with food coloring, if desired.

Holiday Wreaths

½ cup margarine or butter
1 package (10 ounces, about 40) regular marshmallows
1 teaspoon green liquid food coloring
6 cups KELLOGG'S® CORN FLAKES® cereal
Red cinnamon candies

1. Melt margarine in large saucepan over low heat. Add marshmallows and cook, stirring constantly, until marshmallows melt and mixture is syrupy. Remove from heat. Stir in food coloring.

2. Add Kellogg's Corn Flakes® cereal. Stir until well coated.

3. Portion warm cereal mixture using ¼ cup dry measure onto wax paper-lined baking sheet. Using buttered fingers, quickly shape mixture into individual wreaths. Dot with red cinnamon candies. *Makes 16 wreaths*

Variation: Press warm cereal mixture into buttered 5½-cup ring mold or shape into ring on serving plate. Remove from mold and dot with red candies. Slice to serve.

Christmas Tree Cookies

1 package DUNCAN HINES® Golden Sugar Cookie Mix
2 eggs
⅓ cup vegetable oil
Green food coloring
½ cup sliced natural almonds
Pecan halves, cut in half
Red candied cherries, cut in fourths

1. Preheat oven to 375°F. Combine cookie mix, eggs, oil and 4 to 5 drops green food coloring in large bowl. Stir until thoroughly blended. Form dough into pea-size balls. Place 15 balls with sides touching in triangle shape on ungreased baking sheet. Repeat, placing cookies 2 inches apart.

2. Insert almonds between balls to form branches. Place 1 pecan piece in bottom of each tree to form trunk. Place 1 cherry piece on top ball of each tree. Bake at 375°F for 7 to 8 minutes or until set. Cool 1 minute on baking sheets. Remove to cooling racks.
Makes 2 dozen cookies

Angels

1 recipe Butter Cookie
     Dough (recipe follows)
1 egg, lightly beaten
     Small pretzels, white
     frosting, toasted
     coconut, edible glitter
     dust and assorted
     small decors

1. Prepare Butter Cookie
Dough. Refrigerate about
6 hours or until firm.

2. Preheat oven to 350°F.
Grease cookie sheets. Roll
dough on floured surface to
¼-inch thickness. Cut out 12
(4-inch) triangles. Reroll scraps
to ¼-inch thickness. Cut out
12 (1½-inch) circles.

3. Place triangles on prepared
cookie sheets. Brush with
beaten egg. Attach circle,
pressing gently.

4. Bake 8 to 10 minutes or just
until edges begin to brown.
Remove to wire racks; cool
completely.

5. Attach pretzels to back of
each cookie for wings using
frosting as "glue." Let dry

30 minutes. Pipe frosting
around hairline of each angel;
sprinkle with coconut and
glitter dust.

6. Pipe frosting on body of
cookie to resemble arms and
gown. Decorate faces as
desired. Let stand 1 hour or
until dry.

Makes 1 dozen cookies

Butter Cookie Dough

 ¾ cup butter, softened
 ¼ cup granulated sugar
 ¼ cup packed light brown
     sugar
 1 egg yolk
1¾ cups all-purpose flour
 ¾ teaspoon baking powder
 ⅛ teaspoon salt

1. Combine butter, granulated
sugar, brown sugar and egg
yolk in medium bowl. Add
flour, baking powder and salt;
mix well.

2. Cover; refrigerate about
4 hours or until firm.

Candy Cane Cookies

1 cup sugar
⅔ cup margarine, softened
½ cup egg substitute
2 teaspoons vanilla extract
1 teaspoon almond extract
3 cups all-purpose flour
1 teaspoon DAVIS® Baking Powder
½ teaspoon red food coloring

1. Beat sugar and margarine in large bowl with mixer at medium speed until creamy. Beat in egg substitute, vanilla and almond extracts.

2. Mix flour and baking powder in small bowl; stir into margarine mixture.

3. Divide dough in half; tint half with red food coloring. Wrap each half and refrigerate at least 2 hours.

4. Divide each half into 32 pieces. Roll each piece into 5-inch rope. Twist 1 red and 1 white rope together and bend 1 end to form candy cane shape. Place on ungreased baking sheets.

5. Bake in preheated 350°F oven for 8 to 10 minutes or just until set and lightly golden. Remove from sheets; cool on wire racks. Store in airtight container.   *Makes 32 cookies*

Prep Time: 20 minutes
Chill Time: 2 hours
Cook Time: 8 minutes
Total Time: 2 hours and 28 minutes

Helpful Hint

Most cookies freeze well for several months. Store unfrosted cookies in sealed plastic bags or airtight containers with plastic wrap or waxed paper between layers of cookies. Most cookies thaw at room temperature in 10 to 15 minutes.

Almond Milk Chocolate Chippers

½ cup slivered almonds
1¼ cups all-purpose flour
½ teaspoon baking soda
½ teaspoon salt
½ cup butter, softened
½ cup firmly packed light brown sugar
⅓ cup granulated sugar
1 large egg
2 tablespoons water
½ teaspoon almond extract
1 cup milk chocolate chips

1. Preheat oven to 350°F. To toast almonds, spread on baking sheet. Bake 8 to 10 minutes or until golden brown, stirring frequently. Remove almonds from pan and cool; set aside.

2. *Increase oven temperature to 375°F.* Combine flour, baking soda and salt in small bowl.

3. Beat butter, brown sugar and granulated sugar in large bowl until light and fluffy. Beat in egg until well blended. Beat in liqueur. Gradually add flour mixture. Beat until well blended. Stir in chips and almonds.

4. Drop dough by rounded teaspoonfuls 2 inches apart onto ungreased cookie sheets.

5. Bake 9 to 10 minutes or until edges are golden brown. Let cookies stand on cookie sheets 2 minutes. Remove cookies to wire racks; cool completely. Store tightly covered at room temperature or freeze up to 3 months.
Makes about 3 dozen cookies

Holiday Cookies on a Stick

1 cup (2 sticks) butter or
  margarine, softened
¾ cup granulated sugar
¾ cup packed light brown
  sugar
1 teaspoon vanilla extract
2 eggs
2⅓ cups all-purpose flour
½ cup HERSHEY'S Cocoa
1 teaspoon baking soda
½ teaspoon salt
  About 8 wooden ice
  cream sticks
1 tub (16 ounces) vanilla
  ready-to-spread
  frosting (optional)
  Decorating icing in tube,
  colored sugar, candy
  sprinkles, HERSHEY'S
  Holiday Candy Coated
  Bits, HERSHEY'S MINI
  KISSES™ Semi-Sweet
  or Milk Chocolate
  Baking Pieces

1. Heat oven to 350°F.

2. Beat butter, granulated sugar, brown sugar and vanilla in large bowl on medium speed of mixer until creamy. Add eggs; beat well. Stir together flour, cocoa, baking soda and salt; gradually add to butter mixture, beating until well blended.

3. Drop dough by scant ¼ cupfuls onto ungreased cookie sheet, about 3 inches apart. Shape into balls. Insert wooden stick about three-fourths of the way into side of each ball. Flatten slightly.

4. Bake 8 to 10 minutes or until set. (Cookies will spread during baking.) Cool 3 minutes; using wide spatula, carefully remove from cookie sheet to wire rack. Cool completely.

5. Spread with frosting, if desired. Decorate as desired with Christmas motifs, such as star, tree, candy cane, holly and Santa using decorating icing and garnishes.

Makes about 8 (3½-inch) cookies

Holiday Cookies on a Stick

Gingerbread Bears

3½ cups all-purpose flour
2 teaspoons ground cinnamon
1½ teaspoons ground ginger
1 teaspoon salt
1 teaspoon baking soda
1 teaspoon ground allspice
1 cup butter, softened
1 cup firmly packed brown sugar
1 teaspoon vanilla
⅓ cup molasses
2 eggs
Assorted cookie nonpareils (optional)
Ornamental Frosting (recipe page 55) or prepared creamy or gel-type frostings in tubes (optional)
Colored sugar, assorted candies and grated chocolate (optional)

Place flour, cinnamon, ginger, salt, baking soda and allspice in medium bowl; stir to combine. Set aside. Beat butter, sugar and vanilla in large bowl with electric mixer at medium speed about 5 minutes or until light and fluffy. Beat in molasses and eggs until well blended. Beat in flour mixture at low speed until well blended. Divide dough into 3 equal portions; cover and refrigerate at least 2 hours or up to 24 hours.

Preheat oven to 350°F. Grease large cookie sheets; set aside. Working with 1 portion at a time, roll out dough on lightly floured surface to ⅛-inch thickness. Cut out dough with 3-inch bear-shaped cookie cutter. Place cookies 1 inch apart on prepared cookie sheets. Roll dough scraps into balls and ropes to make eyes and noses and to decorate bears. Decorate bears with nonpareils, if desired. Bake 10 minutes or until bottoms of cookies are golden brown. Let stand on cookie sheets 1 minute. Remove cookies to wire rack; cool completely.

Prepare Ornamental Frosting, if desired. Pipe or spread frosting on cooled cookies to decorate. Decorate with assorted nonpareils, colored sugar, assorted candies and/or grated chocolate, if desired. Store tightly covered at room temperature.
Makes about 3½ dozen cookies

Ornamental Frosting

½ cup butter or margarine, softened
1 teaspoon vanilla
1 package (16 ounces) powdered sugar, sifted
2 tablespoons milk

Beat butter and vanilla in large bowl with electric mixer at medium speed. Beat in powdered sugar and enough milk at low speed until frosting is of desired spreading consistency.

Makes about 2 cups

Helpful Hint

It is best to store decorated cookies in single layers between sheets of waxed paper.

Peanut Butter Chocolate Chippers

1 cup creamy or chunky peanut butter
1 cup firmly packed light brown sugar
1 large egg
¾ cup milk chocolate chips
Granulated sugar

1. Preheat oven to 350°F.

2. Combine peanut butter, brown sugar and egg in medium bowl; mix until well blended. Add chips; mix well.

3. Roll heaping tablespoonfuls of dough into 1½-inch balls. Place balls 2 inches apart on ungreased cookie sheets.

4. Dip table fork into granulated sugar; press criss-cross fashion onto each ball, flattening to ½-inch thickness.

5. Bake 12 minutes or until set. Let cookies stand on cookie sheets 2 minutes. Remove cookies with spatula to wire racks; cool completely.

Makes about 2 dozen cookies

Ice Skates

½ cup (1 stick) butter, softened
1 ¼ cups honey
1 cup packed brown sugar
1 egg, separated
5 ½ cups self-rising flour
1 teaspoon ground ginger
1 teaspoon ground cinnamon
½ cup milk
Cookie Glaze (recipe follows)
Assorted candies and small candy canes

1. Beat butter, honey, sugar and egg yolk in large bowl at medium speed of electric mixer until light and fluffy.

2. Combine flour, ginger and cinnamon in small bowl. Add alternately with milk to butter mixture; beat just until combined. Cover; refrigerate 30 minutes.

3. Preheat oven to 350°F. Grease cookie sheets.

4. Roll out dough on lightly floured surface to ¼-inch thickness. Cut out cookies using 3½-inch boot-shaped cookie cutter. Place cookies 2 inches apart on prepared cookie sheets.

5. Bake 8 to 10 minutes or until lightly browned. Cool 2 minutes on cookie sheets. Remove to wire rack; cool completely.

6. Decorate cookies with colored icings and candies as shown in photo.
Makes about 4 dozen cookies

Cookie Glaze

4 cups powdered sugar
4 to 6 tablespoons milk
Assorted food coloring

Combine powdered sugar and enough milk to make a medium-thick pourable glaze. Tint with food coloring as desired.   *Makes about 4 cups*

Star Christmas Tree Cookies

COOKIES
- ½ cup vegetable shortening
- ⅓ cup butter or margarine, softened
- 2 egg yolks
- 1 teaspoon vanilla extract
- 1 package DUNCAN HINES® Moist Deluxe Yellow or Devil's Food Cake Mix
- 1 tablespoon water

FROSTING
- 1 container (16 ounces) DUNCAN HINES® Vanilla Frosting
- Green food coloring
- Red and green sugar crystals for garnish
- Assorted colored candies and decors for garnish

Preheat oven to 375°F. For Cookies, combine shortening, butter, egg yolks and vanilla extract. Blend in cake mix gradually. Add 1 teaspoonful water at a time until dough is rolling consistency. Divide dough into 4 balls. Flatten one ball with hand; roll to ⅛-inch thickness on lightly floured surface. Cut with graduated star cookie cutters. Repeat using remaining dough. Bake large cookies together on *ungreased* baking sheet. Bake 6 to 8 minutes or until edges are light golden brown. Cool cookies 1 minute. Remove from baking sheet. Repeat with smaller cookies, testing for doneness at minimum baking time.

For Frosting, tint vanilla frosting with green food coloring. Frost cookies and stack beginning with largest cookies on bottom and ending with smallest cookies on top. Rotate cookies when stacking to alternate corners. Decorate as desired with colored sugar crystals, assorted colored candies and decors.

Makes 2 to 3 dozen cookies

Graham Peanut Butter Crunchies

1 Butter Flavor* CRISCO®
  Stick or 1 cup Butter
  Flavor CRISCO® all-
  vegetable shortening
1 cup extra crunchy peanut
  butter
1 cup firmly packed brown
  sugar
1 cup granulated sugar
2 eggs
1 teaspoon vanilla
2 cups all-purpose flour
2 teaspoons baking soda
½ teaspoon salt
1 cup graham cracker
  crumbs
⅓ cup milk

*Butter Flavor Crisco is artificially flavored.

1. Heat oven to 350°F. Place sheets of foil on countertop for cooling cookies.

2. Combine shortening, peanut butter, brown sugar and granulated sugar in large bowl. Beat at medium speed of electric mixer until well blended. Beat in eggs and vanilla.

3. Combine flour, baking soda and salt. Mix into creamed mixture at low speed until just blended. Stir in crumbs and milk.

4. Form dough into 1-inch balls. Place 2 inches apart on ungreased baking sheet. Make crisscross pattern on dough with floured fork.

5. Bake at 350°F 10 to 11 minutes, or until edges of cookies are lightly browned. *Do not overbake.* Remove cookies to foil to cool completely.

Makes about 6 dozen cookies

Helpful Hint

If you don't have graham cracker crumbs on hand, make your own! Crush whole crackers quickly and easily by placing them in a sealed plastic food storage bag. Then, run a rolling pin over the bag several times to pulverize them.

Mystical Layered Bars

⅓ cup butter
1 cup graham cracker crumbs
½ cup uncooked old-fashioned or quick oats
1 can (14 ounces) sweetened condensed milk
1 cup flaked coconut
¾ cup semisweet chocolate chips
¾ cup raisins
1 cup coarsely chopped pecans

Preheat oven to 350°F. Melt butter in 13×9-inch baking pan. Remove from oven.

Sprinkle graham cracker crumbs and oats evenly over butter; press with fork. Drizzle condensed milk over oats. Layer coconut, chocolate chips, raisins and pecans over milk.

Bake 25 to 30 minutes or until lightly browned. Cool in pan on wire rack 5 minutes; cut into 2×1½-inch bars. Cool completely in pan on wire rack. Store tightly covered at room temperature or freeze up to 3 months.   *Makes 3 dozen bars*

Lemony Butter Cookies

½ cup butter, softened
½ cup sugar
1 egg
1½ cups all-purpose flour
2 tablespoons lemon juice
1 teaspoon grated lemon peel
½ teaspoon baking powder
⅛ teaspoon salt
Additional sugar

Beat butter and sugar in large bowl with electric mixer until creamy. Beat in egg until light and fluffy. Mix in flour, lemon juice and peel, baking powder and salt. Cover; refrigerate about 2 hours or until firm.

Preheat oven to 350°F. Roll out small portion of dough, on well-floured surface, to ¼-inch thickness. (Keep remaining dough in refrigerator.) Cut with 3-inch round cookie cutter. Transfer to ungreased cookie sheets. Sprinkle with sugar.

Bake 8 to 10 minutes or until lightly browned on edges. Cool 1 minute on cookie sheets. Remove to wire racks; cool completely.
    Makes about 2½ dozen cookies

Tasteful Gifts

Frosted Peanut Butter Peanut Brittle Cookies

PEANUT BRITTLE
1½ cups granulated sugar
1½ cups shelled unroasted Spanish peanuts
¾ cup light corn syrup
½ teaspoon salt
1 tablespoon Butter Flavor* CRISCO® Stick or 1 tablespoon Butter Flavor CRISCO® all-vegetable shortening plus additional for greasing
1½ teaspoons vanilla
1½ teaspoons baking soda

COOKIES
½ Butter Flavor CRISCO® Stick or ½ cup Butter Flavor CRISCO® all-vegetable shortening
½ cup granulated sugar
½ cup packed brown sugar
½ cup creamy peanut butter
1 tablespoon milk
1 egg
1⅓ cups all-purpose flour
¾ teaspoon baking soda
½ teaspoon baking powder
¼ teaspoon salt

TOPPING
1¼ cups peanut butter chips
1 cup reserved crushed peanut brittle

continued on page 64

Frosted Peanut Butter Peanut Brittle Cookies

Frosted Peanut Butter Peanut Brittle Cookies, continued

1. For peanut brittle, grease 15½×12-inch baking sheet with shortening.

2. Combine 1½ cups granulated sugar, nuts, corn syrup and ½ teaspoon salt in 3-quart saucepan. Cook and stir on medium-low heat until 240°F on candy thermometer.

3. Stir in 1 tablespoon shortening and vanilla. Cook and stir until 300°F on candy thermometer. *Watch closely so mixture does not burn.*

4. Remove from heat. Stir in 1½ teaspoons baking soda. Pour onto prepared baking sheet. Spread to ¼-inch thickness. Cool. Break into pieces. Crush into medium-fine pieces to measure 1 cup.

5. For cookies, heat oven to 375°F. Place sheets of foil on countertop for cooling cookies.

6. Combine ½ cup shortening, ½ cup granulated sugar, brown sugar, peanut butter and milk in large bowl. Beat until well blended. Beat in egg.

7. Combine flour, ¾ teaspoon baking soda, baking powder and ¼ teaspoon salt. Add gradually at low speed. Mix until well blended.

8. Shape dough into 1¼-inch balls. Place 3½ inches apart on ungreased baking sheet. Flatten into 3-inch circles.

9. Bake for 8 to 9 minutes or until light brown. *Do not overbake.* Cool 2 minutes on baking sheet. Remove cookies to foil to cool completely.

10. For topping, place peanut butter chips in microwave-safe bowl. Microwave at 50% (MEDIUM). Stir after 1 minute. Repeat until smooth (or melt in saucepan on very low heat). Spread over half of each cookie.

11. Sprinkle reserved crushed peanut brittle over topping. Refrigerate to set quickly or let stand at room temperature.

Makes 2 dozen cookies

Chocolate Mint Sandwiches

2 squares (1 ounce each) unsweetened chocolate
½ cup butter, softened
1 cup packed light brown sugar
1 egg
1 teaspoon vanilla
⅛ teaspoon baking soda
2 cups all-purpose flour
Creamy Mint Filling (recipe follows)

Melt chocolate in top of double boiler over hot, not boiling, water. Remove from heat; cool. Cream butter and brown sugar in large bowl. Beat in egg, melted chocolate, vanilla and baking soda until light and fluffy. Stir in flour to make stiff dough. Divide dough into four parts. Shape each part into a roll about 1½ inches in diameter. Wrap in plastic wrap; refrigerate at least 1 hour or up to 2 weeks. (For longer storage, freeze up to 6 weeks.)

Preheat oven to 375°F. Cut rolls into ⅛-inch-thick slices; place 2 inches apart on ungreased cookie sheets. Bake 6 to 7 minutes or until firm. Remove to wire racks to cool. Prepare Creamy Mint Filling. Spread filling on bottoms of half the cookies. Top with remaining cookies, bottom sides down.

Makes about 3 dozen sandwich cookies

Creamy Mint Filling

2 tablespoons butter or margarine, softened
1½ cups powdered sugar
3 to 4 tablespoons light cream or half-and-half
¼ teaspoon peppermint extract
Few drops green food coloring

Cream butter with powdered sugar and cream in small bowl until smooth and blended. Stir in peppermint extract and food coloring; blend well.

Welsh Tea Cakes

¾ **cup chopped dried mixed fruit or fruit bits or golden raisins**
2 **tablespoons warm water**
2¼ **cups all-purpose flour**
2½ **teaspoons ground cinnamon, divided**
1 **teaspoon baking powder**
½ **teaspoon baking soda**
¼ **teaspoon salt**
¼ **teaspoon ground cloves**
1 **cup butter, softened**
1¼ **cups sugar, divided**
1 **egg**
⅓ **cup sliced almonds (optional)**

1. Preheat oven to 375°F.

2. Combine dried fruit and water in medium bowl; let sit at least 10 minutes to plump.

3. Place flour, 1½ teaspoons cinnamon, baking powder, baking soda, salt and cloves in medium bowl; stir to combine.

4. Beat butter and 1 cup sugar in large bowl with electric mixer at medium speed until light and fluffy. Beat in egg. Gradually add flour mixture. Beat at low speed until well blended. Stir in fruit with water using spoon.

5. Combine remaining ¼ cup sugar and 1 teaspoon cinnamon in small bowl. Roll heaping teaspoonfuls of dough into 1-inch balls; roll balls in cinnamon sugar to coat. Place balls 2 inches apart on ungreased cookie sheets.

6. Press balls to ¼-inch thickness using bottom of glass dipped in granulated sugar. Press 3 almond slices horizontally into center of each cookie. (Almonds will spread evenly and flatten upon baking.)

7. Bake 10 to 12 minutes or until lightly browned. Remove tea cakes with spatula to wire racks; cool completely.

8. Store tightly covered at room temperature or freeze up to 3 months.
   Makes about 3½ dozen cookies

Festive Lebkuchen

3 tablespoons butter
1 cup packed brown sugar
¼ cup honey
1 egg
  Grated peel and juice of
    1 lemon
3 cups all-purpose flour
2 teaspoons ground allspice
½ teaspoon baking soda
½ teaspoon salt
  Prepared white icing

Melt butter with brown sugar and honey in medium saucepan over low heat, stirring constantly. Pour into large bowl. Cool 30 minutes. Add egg, lemon peel and juice; beat 2 minutes with electric mixer on high speed. Stir in flour, allspice, baking soda and salt until well blended. Cover; refrigerate overnight or up to 3 days.

Preheat oven to 350°F. Grease cookie sheet. Roll out dough to ½-inch thickness on lightly floured surface with lightly floured rolling pin. Cut out with 3-inch cookie cutter. Transfer to prepared cookie sheet. Bake 15 to 18 minutes until edges are light brown.

Cool 1 minute. Remove to wire rack; cool completely. Decorate with white icing. Store in airtight container.

Makes 1 dozen cookies

Helpful Hint

Chilled cookie dough is easier to handle when making cutouts. Remove only enough dough from the refrigerator to work with at one time. Save any trimmings and reroll them together to prevent the dough from becoming tough. To minimize sticking of dough when using cookie cutters, dip cutters in flour or spray with vegetable spray.

Rugelach

1½ cups all-purpose flour
¼ teaspoon salt
¼ teaspoon baking soda
½ cup butter, softened
1 package (3 ounces) cream cheese, softened
⅓ cup plus ¼ cup granulated sugar, divided
1 teaspoon grated lemon peel, divided
1 cup ground toasted walnuts
1 teaspoon ground cinnamon
2 tablespoons honey
1 tablespoon lemon juice
Powdered sugar

Combine flour, salt and baking soda in small bowl.

Beat butter, cream cheese, ⅓ cup granulated sugar and ½ teaspoon lemon peel in large bowl with electric mixer at medium speed about 5 minutes or until light and fluffy. Slowly add flour mixture. Beat at low speed until well blended.

Form dough into three 5-inch discs; wrap in plastic wrap and refrigerate until firm, about 2 hours.

Preheat oven to 375°F. Grease cookie sheet; set aside.

Combine walnuts, remaining ¼ cup granulated sugar and cinnamon in medium bowl; set aside. Combine honey, remaining ½ teaspoon lemon peel and lemon juice in small bowl; set aside.

Working with 1 piece of dough at a time, remove plastic wrap and place dough on lightly floured surface. Roll out dough with lightly floured rolling pin to 10-inch circle. Keep remaining dough refrigerated.

Brush with ⅓ of honey mixture. Sprinkle with ⅓ cup nut mixture. Lightly press into dough.

Cut circle into 12 triangles Beginning with wide end of triangle, tightly roll up, jelly-roll fashion. Place cookies 1 inch apart on cookie sheet.

Repeat with 2 remaining dough pieces and filling ingredients. Bake 10 to 12 minutes or until lightly golden brown. Let cookies stand on cookie sheets 1 minute. Remove cookies to wire rack; cool completely. Sprinkle with powdered sugar.

Makes 3 dozen cookies

Festive Cranberry Cheese Bars

2 cups all-purpose flour
1½ cups oats
1 cup (2 sticks) butter or margarine, softened
¾ cup plus 1 tablespoon firmly packed brown sugar, divided
1 (8-ounce) package cream cheese, softened
1 (14-ounce) can EAGLE® BRAND Sweetened Condensed Milk (NOT evaporated milk)
¼ cup REALEMON® Lemon Juice From Concentrate
1 (16-ounce) can whole berry cranberry sauce
2 tablespoons cornstarch

1. Preheat oven to 350°F. Grease 13×9-inch baking pan. In large bowl, beat flour, oats, butter and ¾ cup sugar until crumbly. Reserve 1½ cups crumb mixture. Press remaining crumb mixture on bottom of prepared pan. Bake 15 minutes or until lightly browned.

2. Meanwhile, in medium bowl, beat cream cheese until fluffy. Gradually beat in **Eagle Brand** until smooth; stir in **ReaLemon**. Spread over baked crust. Combine cranberry sauce, cornstarch and remaining 1 tablespoon sugar. Spoon over cheese layer. Top with reserved crumb mixture.

3. Bake 45 minutes or until golden. Cool and cut into bars. Store covered in refrigerator.

Makes 24 to 36 bars

Prep Time: 25 minutes
Bake Time: 60 minutes

Helpful Hint

For a great holiday dessert, cut these bars into large squares and serve them warm, topped with ice cream.

Chocolate Nut Slices

¾ **Butter Flavor CRISCO®
  Stick or ¾ cup Butter
  Flavor CRISCO® all-
  vegetable shortening**
½ **cup granulated sugar**
⅓ **cup packed brown sugar**
2 **tablespoons milk**
1½ **teaspoons vanilla**
1 **egg**
1¼ **cups all-purpose flour**
⅓ **cup unsweetened cocoa
  powder**
½ **teaspoon baking soda**
½ **teaspoon salt**
¾ **cup chopped pecans**
½ **cup semi-sweet chocolate
  chips**

DRIZZLE
½ **teaspoon Butter Flavor
  CRISCO® Stick or ½
  teaspoon Butter Flavor
  CRISCO® all-vegetable
  shortening**
½ **cup white melting
  chocolate, chopped**
Chopped pecans

1. Heat oven to 350°F. Place sheets of foil on countertop.

2. For cookie, combine shortening, granulated sugar, brown sugar, milk and vanilla in large bowl. Beat at medium speed of electric mixer until well blended. Beat in egg.

3. Combine flour, cocoa, baking soda and salt. Mix into creamed mixture at low speed until blended. Stir in nuts and chocolate chips.

4. Divide dough into 4 equal portions. Form each into 1×8-inch roll on waxed paper. Lift ends of waxed paper and roll dough to get a nicely shaped roll. Place 3 inches apart on ungreased baking sheet.

5. Bake at 350°F for 10 minutes, or until set. *Do not overbake.* Cool 2 minutes on baking sheet. Remove cookies to foil to cool completely.

6. For drizzle, combine shortening and white chocolate; microwave for 1 minute at 50% (MEDIUM) in microwave-safe cup. Stir; repeating until smooth. Drizzle over cooled cookie. Sprinkle with nuts.

7. Cut diagonally into 1-inch slices.

Makes about 3 dozen cookies

Acknowledgments

The publisher would like to thank the companies and organizations listed below for the use of their recipes and photographs in this publication.

Bestfoods

Dole Food Company, Inc.

Duncan Hines® and Moist Deluxe® are registered trademarks of Aurora Foods Inc.

Eagle® Brand

Eggbeaters®

Hershey Foods Corporation

Kellogg Company

Kraft Foods Holdings

Lipton®

Nabisco Biscuit Company

Nestlé USA, Inc.

The Procter & Gamble Company

Sokol and Company

Index

METRIC CONVERSION CHART

VOLUME MEASUREMENTS (dry)

$^1/_8$ teaspoon = 0.5 mL
$^1/_4$ teaspoon = 1 mL
$^1/_2$ teaspoon = 2 mL
$^3/_4$ teaspoon = 4 mL
1 teaspoon = 5 mL
1 tablespoon = 15 mL
2 tablespoons = 30 mL
$^1/_4$ cup = 60 mL
$^1/_3$ cup = 75 mL
$^1/_2$ cup = 125 mL
$^2/_3$ cup = 150 mL
$^3/_4$ cup = 175 mL
1 cup = 250 mL
2 cups = 1 pint = 500 mL
3 cups = 750 mL
4 cups = 1 quart = 1 L

VOLUME MEASUREMENTS (fluid)

1 fluid ounce (2 tablespoons) = 30 mL
4 fluid ounces ($^1/_2$ cup) = 125 mL
8 fluid ounces (1 cup) = 250 mL
12 fluid ounces (1$^1/_2$ cups) = 375 mL
16 fluid ounces (2 cups) = 500 mL

WEIGHTS (mass)

$^1/_2$ ounce = 15 g
1 ounce = 30 g
3 ounces = 90 g
4 ounces = 120 g
8 ounces = 225 g
10 ounces = 285 g
12 ounces = 360 g
16 ounces = 1 pound = 450 g

DIMENSIONS

$^1/_{16}$ inch = 2 mm
$^1/_8$ inch = 3 mm
$^1/_4$ inch = 6 mm
$^1/_2$ inch = 1.5 cm
$^3/_4$ inch = 2 cm
1 inch = 2.5 cm

OVEN TEMPERATURES

250°F = 120°C
275°F = 140°C
300°F = 150°C
325°F = 160°C
350°F = 180°C
375°F = 190°C
400°F = 200°C
425°F = 220°C
450°F = 230°C

BAKING PAN SIZES

Utensil	Size in Inches/Quarts	Metric Volume	Size in Centimeters
Baking or	8×8×2	2 L	20×20×5
Cake Pan	9×9×2	2.5 L	23×23×5
(square or	12×8×2	3 L	30×20×5
rectangular)	13×9×2	3.5 L	33×23×5
Loaf Pan	8×4×3	1.5 L	20×10×7
	9×5×3	2 L	23×13×7
Round Layer	8×1½	1.2 L	20×4
Cake Pan	9×1½	1.5 L	23×4
Pie Plate	8×1¼	750 mL	20×3
	9×1¼	1 L	23×3
Baking Dish	1 quart	1 L	—
or Casserole	1½ quart	1.5 L	—
	2 quart	2 L	—